PROWL FOR VOWELS!

The letters **a**, **e**, **i**, **o** ... vowels.
Count the number of ... word
and write the answ... ord.

Practice ...

before ...

The Five ...

1. ant — one
2. noise — three
3. after — two
4. action — three
5. eat — two
6. clearing — three
7. Christmas — two
8. tangerine — four
9. mushroom — three
10. storm — one

Did you beat the clock?

Check your answers!

1. 1 2. 3 3. 2 4. 3 5. 2 6. 3 7. 2 8. 4 9. 3 10. 1

What kind of bird lays electric eggs?
A battery hen!

SOUNDS AMAZING!

Can you list all the words together that rhyme?

Practice question:

pin stop wet

in let pop

_____ _____ _____

The Five Minute Test!

fin top bet tin net mop

forget hop bin fret shop grin

in	**let**	**pop**
bin	forget	top
grin	bet	mop
fin	net	hop
tin	fret	shop

Did you beat the clock?

Check your answers!

in - fin tin bin grin let - bet net forget fret

pop - top mop hop shop

What do you get if you cross a dog with an aeroplane?
A jet setter!

FAT CATS

The letter **a** can make a short sound, such as in 'cat'. Underline the words in each sentence that have this sound.

Practice question:

The fat cat had a snack.

The Five Minute Test!

1. The bats wore green hats.
2. Granny sat on the chair.
3. The man's hand patted the cat.
4. Splat went the sack when it fell on the mat.
5. That is a big bag!
6. Should the band sit or stand?
7. The rat wore the red sash.
8. The black and white van drove to the lake.

Did you beat the clock?

Check your answers!

1. bats, hats 2. Granny, sat 3. man's, hand, patted, cat
4. Splat, sack, mat 5. that, bag 6. band, stand
7. rat, sash 8. black, and, van

What do you get if you cross a cat with a dolphin?
A purr-poise!

FIRST LETTER QUIZ

All the words below start with the letter **d** or the letter **b**. Can you complete them?

Practice question:

_ a m p (a little wet)

The Five Minute Test!

1. _ o g (an animal that barks)
2. _ o l d (brave and not afraid)
3. _ a g (something you carry things in)
4. _ i m (not bright)

5. _ a d (something that is not good)
6. _ e s s e r t (pudding)
7. _ o t t o m (the opposite of top)
8. _ a f t (a little silly)

Did you beat the clock?

Check your answers!

1. dog 2. bold 3. bag 4. dim 5. bad 6. dessert 7. bottom 8. daft

Why did the pony whisper?
Because it was a little hoarse!

MUDDY FUN

The letter **u** can make a short sound, as in 'mud'. Underline the words in each sentence that have this sound.

Practice question:

The boys had fun in the mud.

The Five Minute Test!

1. The girls jumped into the puddles.
2. The cake was cut up into five pieces.
3. The lucky man clung onto the gutter.
4. The cup was used to hold nuts.
5. The sun shone on the ugly duckling.
6. Button up your coat, unless it is warm.
7. The puppies snuggled under the rug.
8. The sticky bun shop is shut on Tuesday.

Did you beat the clock?

Check your answers!

1. jumped, puddles 2. cut, up 3. lucky, clung, gutter
4. cup, nuts 5. sun, ugly, duckling 6. button, up, unless
7. puppies, snuggled, under, rug 8. bun, shut

What do you call a magician who is a secret agent?
James Wand!

M OR N?

All these words begin with either the letter **n** or the letter **m**. Add the missing letter to each word.

Practice question:

_ oan (to complain about things)

The Five Minute Test!

1. _ o o n (appears in the night sky)
2. _ o n e (a word meaning nothing)
3. _ o o n (midday)

4. _ o n e y (another word for cash)
5. _ e a r (close to)

6. _ e a t (flesh of an animal)
7. _ e a t (a tidy room or person)
8. _ o a t (a ditch around a castle)

Did you beat the clock?

Check your answers!

1. moon 2. none 3. noon 4. money
5. near 6. meat 7. neat 8. moat

What happens if a skunk meets the invisible man?
There is an invisible stink!

TOY BOX

Pick the letter **c**, **d**, **p** or **t** to fill in the first letter of the following words. All the words are things you might play with.

Practice question:

_ eck of _ ards

The Five Minute Test!

1. _ eddy
2. _ oll
3. _ ar
4. _ uzzle
5. _ onkers
6. _ ice
7. _ encil
8. _ lay
9. _ ricycle
10. _ aints

Did you beat the clock?

Check your answers!

1. teddy 2. doll 3. car 4. puzzle 5. conkers
6. dice 7. pencil 8. clay 9. tricycle 10. paints

What is another name for parrot food?
Polly filler!

SHORT E QUIZ

The letter **e** can make a short sound, such as in 'red'. Underline the words in each sentence that have this sound.

Practice question:

The hen sat on the nest.

The Five Minute Test!

1. Ken hit his head and went bright red.
2. The man led the rest on his sled.
3. I forget if Ben went east or west.
4. The bed was wet.
5. The tents were set up next to the well.
6. The dreaded spider was caught in its own web.
7. Ten men fled the elephant.
8. The pepper made Jenny sneeze.

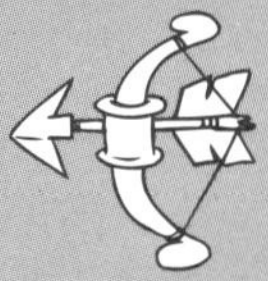

Did you beat the clock?

Check your answers!

1. Ken, head, went, red 2. led, rest, sled 3. forget, Ben, went, west 4. bed, wet 5. tents, set, next, well 6. dreaded, web 7. Ten, men, fled, elephant 8. pepper, Jenny

What do you call a cat who comes top of its class?
Purr-fect!

THE SAME ENDING

The words below can be placed in four groups of rhyming words.
Can you group the words together?

The Five Minute Test!

red	round	sad	bed
sound	fed	find	mad
signed	pound	had	hound
kind	bad	said	mind

________	________	________	________
________	________	________	________
________	________	________	________
________	________	________	________

Did you beat the clock?

Check your answers!

fed red said bed
round pound sound hound

bad sad mad had
signed find kind mind

What do you get if you cross a cow with a pogo stick?
A milk shake!

C OR K?

The letters **k** and **c** often sound the same. Which of the following words start with a **c** and which need a **k**?

Practice question:

_ u t

The Five Minute Test!

1. _ ick

2. _ oat

3. _ een

4. _ eep

5. _ oin

6. _ erb

7. _ ode

8. _ omb

9. _ ing

10. _ aptain

Did you beat the clock?

Check your answers!

1. kick 2. coat 3. keen 4. keep 5. coin 6. kerb
7. code 8. comb 9. king 10. captain

Which Christmas foods sneak around the kitchen?
Mince spies!

HOP AND HOPE

The letter **o** can sound short, as in 'hop', or long, as in 'hope'. Write 'short' or 'long' by each word, according to the sound **o**.

Practice question:

mop _______

The Five Minute Test!

1. rope _________
2. dot _________
3. code _________
4. song _________
5. pocket _________
6. phone _________
7. clock _________
8. focus _________
9. envelope _________
10. poker _________

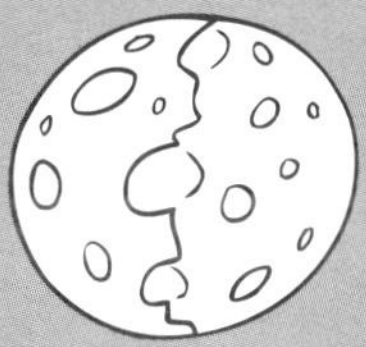

Did you beat the clock?

Check your answers!

1. long 2. short 3. long 4. short 5. short 6. long
7. short 8. long 9. long 10. long

Where do computers learn how to knit sweaters?
On the inter-knit, of course!

COLIN OR CINDY?

The letter **c** can sound like a soft **s**, as in the name Cindy, or it can sound hard, as in Colin. Write 'soft' or 'hard' by each word.

Practice question:

cute _______

The Five Minute Test!

1. cube __________
2. cell __________
3. cage __________
4. cot __________

5. centre __________
6. curtain __________

7. certain __________
8. cereal __________
9. courage __________
10. celebrate __________

Did you beat the clock?

Check your answers!

1. hard 2. soft 3. hard 4. hard 5. soft 6. hard
7. soft 8. soft 9. hard 10. soft

What do vampires like to pour on their dinner?
Grave-y!

LONG OR SHORT?

The letter **i** can sound short, as in 'lick', or long, as in 'like'. Circle 'long' or 'short' depending on the sound **i** makes.

Practice question:

bike long / short

The Five Minute Test!

1.	mine	long / short
2.	dinner	long / short
3.	tide	long / short
4.	sink	long / short
5.	pliers	long / short
6.	night	long / short
7.	fiddle	long / short
8.	mice	long / short
9.	sing	long / short
10.	dried	long / short

Did you beat the clock?

Check your answers!

1. long 2. short 3. long 4. short 5. long 6. long
7. short 8. long 9. short 10. long

What sort of instruments do mice play?
Mouse organs!

RHYME TIME

The words below can be placed in four groups of rhyming words. Can you group the words together?

The Five Minute Test!

bet	trip	forget	grip
fern	need	burn	bleed
debt	clip	seed	earn
slip	net	stern	deed

Did you beat the clock?

Check your answers!

bet debt forget net   slip clip trip grip
bleed deed need seed   earn burn fern stern

Why was the computer in pain?
Because it had slipped a disc!

MOON OR STAR?

Write 'moon' beside the words that contain the **oo** sound. Write 'star' beside the words that contain the **ar** sound.

Practice question:

pool ________

The Five Minute Test!

1. balloon ________

2. large ________

3. stool ________

4. smooth ________

5. market ________

6. room ________

7. farm ________

8. choose ________

9. part ________

10. carthorse ________

Did you beat the clock?

Check your answers!

1. moon 2. star 3. moon 4. moon 5. star 6. moon
7. star 8. moon 9. star 10. star

Waiter, is there soup on the menu today?
No, I wiped it off before we opened!

FAR OR NOT FAR?

Some words with **ar** in their letters rhyme with 'far'. Write 'far' beside the words that rhyme and 'not far' next to ones that don't.

Practice question:

area ________

The Five Minute Test!

1. fear ________
2. park ________
3. earth ________
4. hardly ________
5. cart ________

6. harm ________
7. dear ________
8. argue ________
9. army ________
10. rare ________

Did you beat the clock?

Check your answers!

1. not far 2. far 3. not far 4. far 5. far
6. far 7. not far 8. far 9. far 10. not far

What is an ig?
An eskimo's house without a loo!

SAYING ITS NAME

Say each of the following words out loud to complete this test. Write 'Said it!' next to the words in which the letter **i** says its name.

Practice question:

rip __________

The Five Minute Test!

1. kit __________
2. tried __________
3. pin __________

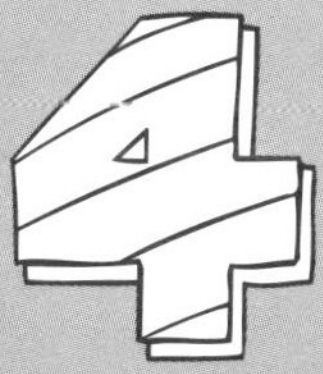

4. ride __________
5. like __________

6. igloo __________
7. hide __________
8. ride __________
9. slipped __________
10. mighty __________

Did you beat the clock?

Check your answers!

2. Said it! 4. Said it! 5. Said it!
7. Said it! 8. Said it! 10. Said it!

How did your brother get that splinter in his finger?
He scratched his head!

SAME LETTERS, DIFFERENT SOUNDS

The letters **ow** can make different sounds.
Do the words below rhyme with 'wow'
or 'blow'? Circle your answers.

Practice question:

cow   low / wow

The Five Minute Test!

1. how   low / wow
2. mow   low / wow
3. flow   low / wow
4. now   low /wow
5. grow   low / wow
6. show   low / wow
7. brow   low / wow
8. crow   low / wow
9. vow   low / wow
10. glow   low / wow

Did you beat the clock?

Check your answers!

1. wow 2. low 3. low 4. wow 5. low 6. low 7. wow
8. low 9. wow 10. low

Where do astronauts park their spaceships?
By parking meteors!

OI, YOU!

The **oi** sound occurs in many words. Can you fill in all the missing letters to complete the **oi** words?

Practice question:

another word for work: _oi_

The Five Minute Test!

1. shiny metal food wrap used in cooking: _ o i _

2. a sharp end of a pencil: _ o i _ _

3. a round disc of money: _ o i _

4. a child with too many presents: _ _o i _ t

5. to heat water in a kettle: _o i _

6. another word for earth in your garden: _ o i _

7. a fuel we get from the earth: o i _

8. to keep away from or not do something: _ _ o i _

Did you beat the clock?

Check your answers!

1. foil 2. point 3. coin 4. spoilt 5. boil 6. soil 7. oil 8. avoid

Why was the flea sad?
Because all its friends had gone to the dogs!

OW AND OU

Can you complete the words in the sentences below? Each incomplete word contains the letters **ow** or **ou**.

Practice question:

The dentist looked into the boy's __ou____

The Five Minute Test!

1. The farmer led his _ows into the barn for milking.
2. The colour of Bill's hair is _ _ow_ .
3. The sky was clear except for one _ _ou_ .
4. On top of his head, the king wears a _ _ow_ .
5. The wind began to _ow_ .
6. The ow_ hoots at midnight.
7. The only thing that moved was a tiny _ou_ _ .
8. Gemma dried herself with the white _ow_ _ .
9. The _ou_ _ was made of bricks.
10. Phil was _ _ou_ of his stamp collection.

Did you beat the clock?

Check your answers!

1. cows 2. brown 3. cloud 4. crown 5. howl 6. owl
7. mouse 8. towel 9. house 10. proud

Waiter: How did you find the steak, sir?
I moved this chip to one side and there it was!

MAKING HAY

Write 'hay' beside the animal words in which **a** makes the sound of its own name.

Practice question:

whale _______

The Five Minute Test!

1. leopard _______
2. mane _______
3. tail _______
4. cheetah _______

5. ladybird _______

6. ant _______
7. gorilla _______
8. plaice _______
9. snake _______
10. shark _______

Did you beat the clock?

Check your answers!

2. hay 3. hay 5. hay
8. hay 9. hay

Which day of the week do eggs hate most?
Fry-day!

ADD A VOWEL

Make 10 new words by placing an extra vowel **after** the vowel in the middle of each word.

Practice question:

set _______

The Five Minute Test!

1. rod _______
2. cot _______
3. bet _______
4. met _______
5. man _______
6. bat _______
7. pond _______
8. spot _______
9. case _______
10. run _______

Did you beat the clock?

Check your answers!

1. road 2. coat 3. beat 4. meat/meet 5. main 6. bait
7. pound 8. spout 9. cause 10. ruin

Who succeeds?
A bird with no teeth!

MAGIC E

Some words can become new words by adding an **e** at the end. Write the new word, or 'No' on each line.

Practice question:

not ________

The Five Minute Test!

1. can ________
2. fan ________
3. kit ________
4. hat ________
5. rip ________
6. fat ________
7. hand ________
8. slat ________
9. fun ________
10. ton ________
11. pip ________
12. hug ________

Did you beat the clock?

Check your answers!

1. cane 2. No 3. kite 4. hate 5. ripe 6. fate
7. No 8. slate 9. No 10. tone 11. pipe 12. huge

Why were the teacher's eyes crossed?
Because she couldn't control her pupils!

HARD G, SOFT G

The letter **g** can make two different sounds: hard, as in 'guard', or soft, as in 'gym'. Write 'soft' or 'hard' beside the following words.

Practice question:

gentle ________

The Five Minute Test!

1. garden ______
2. gentle ______
3. glide ______
4. giant ______
5. goose ______
6. general ______
7. gold ______
8. guest ______
9. germ ______
10. gasp ______

Did you beat the clock?

Check your answers!

1. hard 2. soft 3. hard 4. soft 5. hard 6. soft
7. hard 8. hard 9. soft 10. hard

Why are graveyards so noisy?
Because of all the coffins!

ODD ONE OUT

One word in each row has a different vowel sound to the others. Circle the odd one out in each row.

Practice question:

raid ate hay attic

The Five Minute Test!

1. cower brown mow now
2. flan clan band cane
3. mice twice slick spice
4. scale snail staple apple
5. green great grease greedy
6. pest dressed nest need
7. globe globule drove slow
8. puppet flute cube dune
9. jeep scene seat fret
10. Jane Jake Jack Jade

Did you beat the clock?

Check your answers!

1. mow 2. cane 3. slick 4. apple 5. great
6. need 7. globule 8. puppet 9. fret 10. Jack

What do you get if you cross a hen with a dog?
Pooched eggs!

PH OR F?

The letters **ph** make the sound **f**. Fill in the missing words, which all start with either the letters **ph** or the letter **f**.

Practice question:

The cows ate grass in the f _ _ _ _ .

The Five Minute Test!

1. Andy picked up the ph_ _ _ and dialled Kit's number.
2. There were four f_ _ _ _ boys than girls in the class.
3. The trip cost nothing. It was f_ _ _ .
4. Jan looked for the right ph_ _ _ _ in his French book.
5. The children at Fiona's new school were nice and f_ _ _ _ _ _ _ .
6. The teacher showed Jim a ph_ _ _ he had taken with his camera.
7. The scouts played f_ _ _ _ _ - the - leader.
8. The ph_ _ _ _ _ was a scary sight at the opera house.

Did you beat the clock?

Check your answers!

1. phone 2. fewer 3. free 4. phrase 5. friendly
6. photo 7. follow 8. phantom

Which trees do ghouls like best?
Ceme-trees!

THE SAME BUT DIFFERENT

Circle the correct word from two words that sound the same to complete each sentence.

Practice question:

The old lady looked very pail / pale.

The Five Minute Test!

1. The farmer tied up a bail / bale of hay.
2. The stoat ran around in a days / daze.
3. Anne dyed / died her hair bright orange.
4. The book cost a lot of money. It was very dear / deer.
5. Tom knocked lightly at the window pain / pane.
6. Emma bought her new coat at the winter sale / sail.
7. Paul still felt weak / week after time off for illness.
8. The queue / cue for the opening of the new cinema was long.
9. The seeds were sewn / sown in April.
10. The sole / soul of Jack's shoe was covered in mud.

Did you beat the clock?

Check your answers!

1. bale 2. daze 3. dyed 4. dear 5. pane 6. sale
7. weak 8. queue 9. sown 10. sole

How do you fit more pigs on your farm?
Build a sty-scraper!

STARTERS ORDERS

Add **pl**, **cl** or **sl** in front of each group of letters to make words.

Practice question:

______ ope

The Five Minute Test!

1. ____ imb
2. ____ imy
3. ____ ace
4. ____ oppy
5. ____ ide
6. ____ anet
7. ____ ub
8. ____ umsy
9. ____ astic
10. ____ iers

Did you beat the clock?

Check your answers!

1. climb 2. slimy 3. place 4. sloppy 5. slide 6. planet
7. club 8. clumsy 9. plastic 10. pliers

Why did the turkey cross the road?
To prove he wasn't a chicken!

BEFORE AND AFTER

Add **er** or **re** after the letters below to make words.

Practice question:

play ___

The Five Minute Test!

1. ca ___
2. whe ___
3. fla ___
4. fa ___
5. ste ___
6. sta ___
7. read ___
8. cent ___
9. few ___
10. clev ___

Did you beat the clock?

Check your answers!

1. care 2. where 3. flare 4. fare 5. steer 6. stare
7. reader 8. centre 9. fewer 10. clever

Why is the Mississippi an unusual river?
Because it has four eyes but cannot see!

FIRST LETTER CHALLENGE

Which letter from the list below can be added to each set of letters to make words? Use each letter once.

Practice question:

_ e _ y _ ay

The Five Minute Test!

1. _ est _ ost _ ast
2. _ e _ y _ ine
3. _ asp _ as _ argle
4. _ hisk _ander _afer
5. _ very _ gg _ cho
6. _ ocus _ ort _ riend
7. _ hird _ ruth _ unnel
8. _ oast _ ecent _ ant
9. _ ick _ table _ nake
10. _ lass _ lue _ ard

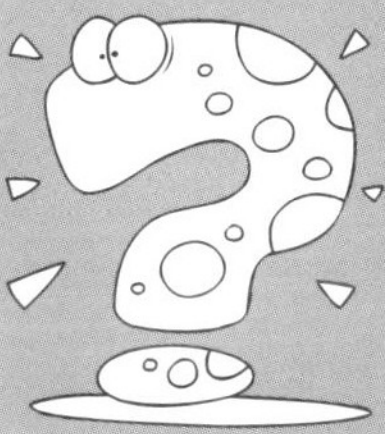

c e f g m p r s t w

Did you beat the clock?

Check your answers!

1. p 2. m 3. g 4. w 5. e 6. f 7. t 8. r 9. s 10. c

What is worse than finding a worm in your apple?
Finding half a worm!

LAST LETTER CHALLENGE

Which letter from the list below can be added to each set of letters to make words? Use each letter once.

Practice question:

noo _   fu _   trai _

The Five Minute Test!

1. fin _   tun _   pol _
2. plu _   tree _   a _
3. mu_   tra_   cla_
4. coa _   shee _   floa _
5. han _   drea _   loa _
6. ru _   sla _   kno _
7. boo _   kic _   rac _
8. ho _   flo _   cro _
9. ca _   afa _   clea _
10. fo _   bo _   o _

b d e k m r s t w x

Did you beat the clock?

Check your answers!

1.e 2.s 3.m 4.t 5.d 6.b 7.k 8.w 9.r 10.x

Why couldn't the animals play cards on Noah's Ark?
Because Noah was sitting on the deck!

SSSSSS EXPRESS

Complete these words by adding **s** followed by another letter.

Practice question:

_ _ oth

The Five Minute Test!

1. _ _ ord
2. _ _ eater
3. _ _ uirrel
4. _ _ ring
5. _ _ owly
6. _ _ ulptor
7. _ _ rawl
8. _ _ ooth
9. _ _ reamed
10. Choose three words from the list above to complete the sentence below.

Someone __________ as the knight advanced __________ with his __________ in his hand.

Did you beat the clock?

Check your answers!

1. sword 2. sweater 3. squirrel 4. string 5. slowly
6. sculptor 7. scrawl 8. smooth 9. screamed
10. screamed, slowly, sword

Why do elephants paint their toenails red?
So they can hide in cherry trees!